Keep Praying God Is Listening

OrangeBooks Publication

Smriti Nagar, Bhilai, Chhattisgarh - 490020

Website: **www.orangebooks.in**

© Copyright, 2022, Author

All rights reserved. No part of this book may be reproduced, stored in a retrieval system, or transmitted, in any form by any means, electronic, mechanical, magnetic, optical, chemical, manual, photocopying, recording or otherwise, without the prior written consent of its writer.

Keep Praying God Is Listening

Kritika Khetarpal Malik

OrangeBooks Publication
www.orangebooks.in

Keep Praying God Is Listening

By Kritika Khetarpal Malik

Special Thanks to my Daadi (Smt. Shanta Khetarpal Ji) for always guiding me & showing me the right path.

&

My Daddy i.e. my grandfather (Late Shri Madan Lal Khetarpal ji)

My papa i.e. my Father-in-Law (Late Shri Randhir Malik ji)

My Nana (Late Shri Vishwanath Mehra Ji) for always showering their blessings and love on me from the heaven.

About The Book

Being very much part of this material world, I find solace, comfort, and peace with God. This book is about prayers. Prayer is communicating with God as you would with a friend, parent, partner, or sibling. God doesn't require us to come to Him with big words or fancy language. He longs to hear what our hearts desire, our worries, and what we're thankful for. The best part of building a bond with God is the absence of judgment. You can be yourself. Nothing is hidden from Him. He knows exactly how you are feeling when nobody else does.

He knows the causes, the reasons, and the things that brought you to this point. He understands because He made you, and He sees the hurt in your heart like nobody else can. No human being has this ability: "And whatever you ask for in prayer, you will receive if you have faith."

For all my worldly needs, I only pray to God because asking humans only brings disappointment, but praying to God gets my material and worldly desires fulfilled.

I got connected to Guru Nanak Dev ji through my grandmother, (Dadi Ma). It was my daily evening ritual during my teenage days to go to my grandmother while she was doing prayer. Through Gurbani and katha, I understood the preaching of Guru Nanak Dev ji and the power of Ardas (prayers). Just as dirt is washed by soap, in the same way, man's evil thoughts may be washed by prayer and meditation. Sinners have turned into saints through prayer. God is the helper of the helpless, the strength of the weak, and the supporter of the fallen. As human beings, we all make mistakes. We all slip up and make mistakes, and that happens on a daily basis. But no matter the storms you are facing or your past, God loves you, and His love is perfect. I am writing this book while going through my toughest phase of life. Through this book, I am encouraging myself and hoping to encourage millions of people to not lose patience and hope. While we may not like the hard circumstances we are stuck in, we can have hope. A day will come when there will be no more tears or pain. It's a small nudge to have faith in the power of prayers and God.

God answers our prayers in four ways:

The first is "Yes." We ask for something; we pray to God, and He says, "Yes, my child. Here it is; I will give you what you asked for."

The second is "No". For a good reason, God tells us, "No, my child, I will not grant your prayer."

The third is "Wait". It is as if God tells us that the time is not right for us to receive what we want. So, He tells us, "Wait, the time is not yet."

The fourth is, "Here is something better." We have asked for one thing, but He grants us something else and says, "Here is something different, something better that I want to give you."

So, keep praying, because He hears you. God's listening right now, and He'll still be listening tomorrow. "One of the main reasons that we lose our enthusiasm is because we become ungrateful, we let what was once a miracle become common to us."

"When God is our strength, we begin to not only see miracles in the lives of others but in our lives as well." E'yen A. Gardner, Chosen One.

I'm sending my love, light, and healing energy through this book.

About The Author

Kritika Khetarpal Malik is an upcoming fashion designer who owns a brand called KRITIKA K. She graduated in 2012 from Jesus and Mary College, Delhi University, and further did her post-graduation in fashion design from the Pearl Academy of Fashion Technology, New Delhi in the year 2015.

She always wanted to write a book, but whenever she sat down to write, she couldn't find relevant content or inspiration to do so and failed many attempts. She did not consider herself a great writer, but part of her always had an urge to write. But recently, she came across this quote: "Keep praying, God is listening." This quote inspired her to write.

Why did it inspire her?

It inspired her because it came as an answer to her prayers; it was like God was saying to have faith; it was an assurance that everything will be okay, as God is there for her in all difficult times. This compelled her to write for all those who are seeking answers to their prayers and have lost hope; whatever she has learned through Gurbani or childhood stories narrated by her elders, and whatever kind of relationship she has shared with God, she has penned it down. It was like God telling her to write about

His glory. She wishes this book would come as an answer to the prayers of all the readers.

Further to make that leap, she says to have a childlike and not a childish perception. The childlike mind does not seek God in an intellectual sense, but rather to experience and enjoy God in everyday life. This allows the childlike mind to seek and experience true spiritual life outside those places where the adult mind might expect to find God. Having said that, this book is straight from her heart, and she says she is grateful to God for this opportunity. Imbued with grace and her practical approach to spirituality and life, her words teach the power of prayers that guide from visualization to realization, from outer chaos to inner light.

P.S. "She is not a contemporary spiritual teacher who is aligned with any particular religion or tradition and won't call herself a true devotee, but she is just a child of Akal Purakh God) and always asking him to shield her from all the challenges."

Contents

- Faith 1
- Accepting Your Mortality 4
- Prayer And Faith Go Hand In Hand 8
- Prayer Can Change Destinies 11
- Prayer Gives Hope 14
- When My Faith Wavers 16
- Action And Prayer Go Hand In Hand 19
- How Karma Works 21
- Teachings 25
- How I am overcoming my spiritual challenges 33
- Quotes For Uplifting Your Mood In Hard Times 45
- For My Readers 48

Faith

I am Kritika Khetarpal Malik, and I am writing this book at the age of 30.

God has been an integral part of my life.

It's all about faith. If you have faith, you can achieve anything. People find God outside of them but forget to look inside. They forget that they themselves are part of God. There is a saying that faith can move mountains. If you have faith in Him, you can actually see and feel Him close to you.

Story of Dhanna Bhagat

I would like to share this beautiful story, which my grandmother told me about Bhagat Dhanna when I was a child. He was a simple farmer. Every day on his way to his fields, he would pass across the house of a pandit who used to do daily rituals and prayers. Dhanna found this very fascinating. One day, the same pandit was offering food to the statue. Out of curiosity, he asked the pandit, "Why are you offering food to a stone?" The pandit got angry and said, "This is not a stone!" This is Thakurji. If He is pleased, all your wishes will come true. You must feed Thakurji first, and only after that should you eat.

Hearing this, Dhanna got very excited and asked. "How can I get a Thakurji?" The pandit was in a hurry. So, he picked up a normal stone off the ground and gave it to Dhanna, saying, "This is your Thakurji." Excited, Dhanna reached home with Thakurji and cleaned his home, making a lovely corner for Thakurji to rest. He cooked some chapati and made some lassi. Offering the simple stone, he said, "Here, Thakurji." I hope you enjoy this food. But naturally, Thakurji didn't eat or drink. It didn't even move. Dhanna thought maybe Thakurji was annoyed with him, so he tried another tone, saying sweetly, "I hope I haven't bothered you." Please eat. This is the tastiest thing. I know how to make it."

All day, Thakurji didn't eat. Dhanna was very hungry, and just because Thakurji didn't eat, he also didn't eat. He begged, cried, got angry, and did everything to convince Thakurji to eat, but nothing worked. The morning came, and Dhanna Ji had not slept or eaten at all. And then the whole next day and night passed again, and Dhanna stayed awake and didn't eat. "I will not eat until you eat," he told Thakurji. He was very adamant. Before morning dawned on the third day, a miracle happened. Dhanna ji's love, devotion, and innocence made God appear disguised as a young man in front of Dhanna ji, who was made of stone, to have the food offered to him by his beloved child.

Young Dhanna was overjoyed. "I knew you would come." From then on, both became extremely close to each other. The young man sang beautiful songs to Dhanna and helped with anything he wanted. The bond was inseparable. They had so much love for each other.

One day, the Panditji walked by Dhanna's hut. Dhanna ran out excitedly. "Panditji, I can't thank you enough.

Thakurji is the best; He sings the most beautiful songs! The Panditji was confused and asked, "Does your Thakurji sing?"

Dhanna said, "Oh, yes, and he makes the best lassi too." And look, he even helps me in the fields. Panditji saw the plough in the field was moving, but the pundit couldn't see anyone driving the cattle. Now both men were confused. Dhanna said, "Why can't you see Thakurji? "

The Panditji asked "How come you can see Thakur Ji?" Bhagat Dhanna said I will ask Thakurji about it. He knows everything, and when Dhanna asked the young man why only he could see Him, the young man explained. Anyone who sincerely meditates on Naam will see me. He said I have not meditated on Naam. How can I see you? The young man touched Dhanna's forehead, and at that moment, he saw all his past lives. He saw that in his past life, Dhanna had obeyed a guru. His guru taught him how to meditate on the Naam. It was his past and present day devotion that allowed him to see Thakurji.

Thus, it was Dhannaji's faith that he met God by worshipping a stone. Without faith, we cannot expect that things would turn out all right for us no matter what the situation might be, and also, without faith, it is impossible to please God; one must believe that He is and that He is a rewarder of those who diligently seek Him.

P.S. If you can seek God through faith, through faith you can achieve anything in life.

Accepting Your Mortality

Death is an unavoidable part of the cycle of life, yet many of us do everything we can to avoid accepting our mortality. But coming to terms with the inevitability of death can help teach us to live more fully in the here and now. In fact, consciousness of our mortality can enable us to cherish every moment of the life we have.

I am really touched by the Bollywood movie Kal Ho Na Ho. The movie teaches us how to seize the day, every day. Sharing two of my favorite dialogues from the movie that hit me hard.

*"Aaj …. Aaj ek hasi aur baant lo, aaj ek dua aur mang lo, aaj ek sapna aur dekh lo, aaj kya pata, kal ho naa ho.

*(Today.... today share one more smile, today pray one more time, today drink one more tear, today live one more life, today see one more dream, and today, who knows, there may be no tomorrow.)

*Haso, jiyo. Muskurao, Kya Pata Kal Ho Naa Ho.

(*laugh, live, smile..today..for who knows there may or may not be tomorrow.)

I know it's easier said than done to live each day as if it were your last, but without frenzy, without pretense, without apathy, let's give it a try. We cannot fully enjoy life without understanding our inevitable death.

One day we are born, one day we'll be dead, and other days we are living. That is what life is; death is the ultimate truth.

Bhagwat Gita says:
"Jatasya hi dhurvo mrityur dhruvam janmamritasya cha tasmad apariharye rthe na tvam shochitum arhasi

Meaning: Death is certain for one who has been born, and rebirth is inevitable for one who has died. Therefore, you should not lament over the inevitable.

The truth is, life is predestined. According to Mahabharat, the place and time of birth as well as death are prewritten. So, as I said, one day we are born, one day we'll be dead, and other days we are living, but living right should be the goal regardless of good or bad. We can't control all the things that happen, but we can change our attitude towards them and, in the process, shape our future and create our most amazing life experiences.

Story of Kisa Gautami
There was a lady named Kisa Gautami whose son had died. Suffering with unending pain, she went from house to house looking for medicine to bring her son back to life. People started thinking that the lady had lost her senses. One day, she met a man who directed her towards Lord Buddha, who could possibly have a solution for her problem. Buddha told her to look for mustard seeds, and the seeds must be procured from a house that had seen no death. Reinstated with hope, Kisa Gautami once again went on a search from house to house, but to her dismay, she could not find mustard seeds from a house that would fulfill Buddha's condition. Disheartened, she sat at the

edge of the road, thus realizing how selfish she had been. She became conscious of the fact that men were mortal and no one could escape the cycle of life. This was exactly what Buddha wanted her to understand. According to Lord Buddha, feelings of grief and sorrow only increase man's pain and suffering, thus deteriorating his health. Death and sorrow are universal and natural processes. They come to every family. Human life is full of trials and suffering, and each person must overcome them. Real wisdom is to accept the inevitability of death and continue the journey of life.

My point is that we must always act with the best of intentions and never let the hurts of the past or the uncertainties of the future consume us. I would like you to do this activity. If tomorrow really was your last day, how would you spend it? Would you still be complaining or nagging about the pointless things, or would you stand up and fight for the things you really want in your life? What would you say to the people you care about? What would you do with the remaining time here? What would failure mean to you? Would you still be scared to fail because you think about the lasting consequences?

I truly believe in this quote by Steve Jobs: "Remembering that you are going to die is the best way I know to avoid the trap of thinking you have something to lose." You are already naked. There is no reason not to follow your heart and your faith in God because feeling pain from problems and stresses won't make a quick fix possible. To live life fully, one must be fearless. One can become fearless when they know that it's God who is in charge, not them. I truly believe an awareness of one's mortality can lead one to wake up and live an authentic, meaningful life. As you quiet your mind, you begin to see the different components of your being and which ones are out of harmony.

In the Bhagavad Gita, Krishna tells Arjuna, "Give me your mind and heart, and you will come to me." It is as if he is saying, "Always think of me, always love me, and I will guide your heart and your actions." Let your love and devotion guide your heart. Let the thinking mind be balanced by the bhakti heart.

Prayer and Faith Go Hand In Hand

Praying to God with a sincere heart and having faith that he, God, is listening and all your prayers will be answered.

Ever since I was a kid, I have believed in the existence of God. I talk to him, fight with him, get angry with him, and express my gratitude to him because I believe he is listening and walking right beside me.

Story about My Prayers & Faith

I still remember when I was 13 years old. At my early adolescent age, I was extremely emotional, sensitive, and not so confident as a person. I am still an emotional person, but I am now learning to balance my emotions. The smallest of things would bother me; for a 13-year-old, being good in academics is a concern, and I was really scared of failing. If somebody said mean things to me, I would take it to heart. I always wanted to be a good child for my parents. All families go through difficult times; even my family was going through such a phase. I was young and thought problems were my fault, though they had nothing to do with me. I felt insecure and bad about myself. One night, with teary eyes, I was praying and talking to Lord Krishna.

I said if Krishnaji, you are listening, then I want to see you. I don't exactly remember now, but that night I was really sad, so I kept on praying, "Please come." I slept while crying that night, and then my prayers were answered. Lord Krishna did come, but he came in my dream. Despite being a 13-year-old, I sometimes slept in my parents' room, but that night, I was sleeping in my room. My room has a small window; through that window, there is a gallery, and Krishnaji was standing there. The gallery of my house was lit by bright white divine light radiating from his back, and there he was standing in his cross-legged, flute pose, calling my name Kritika, "Mai aa gaya hu (Kritika, I have come"). I was peeking through the window of the room while trembling and getting goosebumps; I was so terrified that I couldn't go near Him while He kept calling me. In my dream, I quickly ran to my parents' room to tell them that Krishnaji had come, but they didn't believe me. Everything I felt was so real; I woke up with a jolt, scared and confused, and my body was still trembling. I still had goosebumps, so I ran to my parents' room at around 3 a.m. and slept with them. When I woke up, I just couldn't believe what had happened—Krishnaji had actually given me His darshan. One thing I learned from this experience is that when you think about Krishna with a pure heart, He will surely come to you. It was because of my faith in Him that He gave His darshan through my dream.

P.S. This is real, not my imagination.

Contrary to what most people think, what moves God to action isn't a prayer. Prayer is not to instruct God, inform God, or impress God. Prayer moves you and me. It is faith that moves God's hand. The value of prayers is twofold. First, prayers activate your faith. Prayer isn't based on how long or how short you pray, but that your prayer is faith-based. Faith says, "I believe and I receive." Just think about it. How are you going to come to God and ask him for something without even knowing, caring about, or believing in Him? What if we walk up to a stranger in a store and tell them to give me a Rs. 500 note? No, I don't know them, but I need a Rs. 500 note, so let me ask just in case he may give it to me. Don't do God like a hat; don't just have your hand out and pray for the sake of it; pray because you have faith in God and what God can do for you.

So many times we give our concerns to God through prayer and we STILL worry about them. That is where your faith comes in again. Even if you are going through a hard time, worried, and/or anxious about something; once you pray and give it to God let it go.

If you pray about something and continue to worry that means you are lacking faith. If you believe that God can answer the prayer, then why worry about it?

If you continue to worry about something that you have prayed about then you are doubting that God is going to come through for you.

Prayer Can Change Destinies

The Earthquake Vs the Power of Prayer

I want to share this story that I came across online by Ravi Kumar Khalsa. There was once a man who did not believe in prayer. He never prayed about anything, but whenever someone would talk about prayer, he would say, "Ah, prayer. If you don't do anything, I'll tell you what prayer is. It's just a big waste of time."

One day, this man was eating a delicious dinner his wife and kids had cooked. "Mmmm, this is yummy, I like this food." All of a sudden, the ground started to shake under their feet.

The whole house rumbled. Even the walls of the house began to shake. Pictures fell off the walls, and dishes fell all over the table and smashed to pieces on the floor. He realized that it was an earthquake and said, "Oh no! We must get out of the house immediately. He gathered his kids, and the whole family tried to make their way through the chaos. The floors began to crack, everything fell out of the cupboards, and the window started to break. Even the walls started to fall. "Oh No?" They cried out. They tried to escape from the house, but it didn't look like they were going to make it. "I don't know if we can survive this!" he cried out, and just then something erupted from the man's heart.

He said a prayer on the spot: "Oh God, save me! My dear Lord, show me your grace!"

The earthquake settled down. Somehow they had all survived. The father had cuts and bruises on his body. His wife was very scared. She was also hurt. "Oh, my wife, you are hurt. I'm also hurt". She interrupted him, "Our children, my poor babies, are in the hospital with broken legs. Our house is half destroyed. How could it get worse than this?"

They both felt really bad: "We barely made it out alive. Everything is ruined, just ruined. Ahhh, this is awful!" She was crying, and he felt desperate and sad. He went outside and looked upwards, and they said, "Oh, you who live in the sky! What happened? I never pray to you, but the one time I do, I thank you. I ask you to save me. Look at this disaster. The priest says that it's always good to pray, but why should I bother? You don't listen anyway, do you?"

Just then, big white clouds started to gather in the skies. A heavenly voice spoke out, "My dear child." The man was filled with awe at the power of what was happening. The voice said, "It was pre-written that all your lives were supposed to be lost in this earthquake. Your souls knew this before you were born into this life. Your souls were all meant to leave your bodies together at this time." The man was filled with wonder. A deep understanding of how life works dawned on him. He now understands that there are no accidents.

He smiled and said to himself, "Everything in the universe is perfect!"

But, there was one thing he still didn't understand. He asked, "If there is such a perfect plan going on, why didn't we die? If that was meant to happen, why are we still alive?"

Full of joy, the heavenly voice answered immediately, "Prayer!"

"It is because of your one prayer that the plan has been rearranged." The man felt so humble that he thought, "Wow, I am just so grateful. Thank you."

The joyful voice continued. "Your affairs have been rearranged; a new plan has been framed; a new agreement has been made. You prayed with so much heart and with such great sincerity that your destiny and the destinies of everyone in your family were rewritten." That is the power of prayer.

Prayer Gives Hope

Prayers give you hope to move forward in life and strength to endure the pain that life inflicts. Life often doesn't go as planned, so you and I need to be prepared with an arsenal of prayers for hope when these unexpected circumstances arise. There are times in our lives when our faith in God begins to waver, and during that time we think praying to God is of no help. Anxiety creeps in, and we start panicking. Worrying makes it worse. We try to control our lives, but our only work is to keep doing our karma and surrendering to God, having faith that our prayers are being answered. The moment you lose your faith in God, you will lose your hope, and hope is very important to keep going in life. We will fall seven times, but if we lose hope, we won't even bother to stand up and try eight times. Martin Luther King, Jr. said, "We must accept finite disappointment but never lose infinite hope." "Hope is being able to see that there is light despite all of the darkness." Desmond Tutor. No matter where you are on your journey, that's exactly where you need to be. The next road is always ahead.

OPRAH WINFREY

Just keep going and trust God. Even when you think He is not listening, He is listening. Trust His plans and have faith in your prayers. Hope is powerful and increases our faith as we recognize the ways God is for us and loves us. I would like to share one Bible verse that will help you recall the faithfulness of God:

"For I know the plans I have for you," declares the LORD, "plans to prosper you and not to harm you, plans to give you hope and a future."

When My Faith Wavers

There are times when I question the existence of God, knowing that there is a supreme power, and doubts fill my mind. Then in those moments, I try to recall a story that my grandmother told me about a man who constantly blamed God for all the problems in his life and all the sufferings in the world. So one day he went to a temple and started talking to God's idol. He was so angry at God that he questioned Him, saying, "Every day I pray to you, then why do you not protect me from all the sufferings? You are just an idol. It is so convenient for you to be an idol and watch people worship you, offering you sweets, flowers, and incense sticks. God, you just stand there as an idol and watch." He again asks questions

"Do you even listen to these people?"

"Do you know how difficult it is to be a human?"

"Do you even know what it is to struggle through life?"

While he was complaining and criticizing God, the idol in front of him came alive and said to the man, "If you think that I do nothing, that I am just an idol who stands in front of everybody in the temple and enjoys all the offerings. If you think my task is easy, then why don't you do that for me? Why don't you take my place and become God and help people who come to you for rescue? Will you do it for me? You think I say nothing and do nothing, so you also just stand and watch. Promise me you won't say anything; you will just stand and enjoy all the offerings. The man turns into God, and people come and worship him. He is happy because he is now God.

Then one day a businessman came to the temple and bowed before God to seek his blessings. Unknowingly, he dropped his wallet while he knelt before God. He went and sat in a corner of a temple to meditate. Meanwhile, a beggar entered the temple and cried in front of God that his children are hungry because he is poor and hadn't managed to beg for anything for them in the past two days. He pleaded to God for help. Suddenly he saw the fallen wallet of the businessman and picked it up. The wallet was filled with money. The poor man was overjoyed because he would be able to feed his hungry children with this money. Now a sailor entered to seek blessings before his sea voyage. After he was done meditating, the businessman opened his eyes and saw the sailor standing and praying. Soon after the businessman realized his wallet was missing, there was no one at the temple before the businessman closed his eyes for meditation, so he suspected the sailor of stealing his wallet and called the police to inquire. Now the man disguised as an idol at the temple told the real truth: that it was not the sailor but the poor man who picked up the wallet, which resulted in the beggar being caught and put into jail by the police. God appeared and told the man, "I turned you into me in the form of an idol and asked you not to utter a word because that's what you think I do. Now look at what you did. You ruined my whole plan. The beggar prayed to me to provide some money so he could feed his hungry children. I granted his wish and dropped the businessman's wallet because I knew the loss would not affect him and would reduce his bad deeds. Through this, I wanted to balance the karma of the businessman." So the man asks the God, "What about the sailor? Why was he arrested for the deed he didn't do?" God replied because he prayed for his safety while he was about to board a ship at sea.

I knew the sea was rough and his ship was going to sink; thus, to save his life, I had stopped him from boarding the ship, so I got him arrested that day. Now, do you realize what I do? Rather than crying and cursing me, learn to trust.

Remember, God's vision for your life may be different than yours. Believe that he always has your best interests at heart and that his plans for you are bigger and better than your own. God looks at the bigger picture and sees things you don't see. Lay aside your plans and trust God's plans for your life. Thus, the man realized his mistake.

This story gives me comfort and peace and helps me restore my faith in God. This story has encouraged me at various points in my life to believe that God has a better plan and that he is working on it.

Action and Prayer Go Hand In Hand

Prayer without action is like never putting the vehicle into gear. The engine will keep on running without the car moving forward. On the other hand, action without prayer is like trying to drive a car without fuel. It simply does not work, so a balance has to be struck between prayer and action. They go hand in hand.

You can't just sit. Folding hands and waiting for God to come and do all the work. Just because you prayed, it's you who is going to make efforts; do your praying, Karam, and God will help you on your path.

What I am saying is that if I have my examination tomorrow and I only pray and do not study, then this won't work. God is not going to come and write my examination paper. For that, I have to study, learn, do my karam (actions), and leave the rest to God. I will just pray that you help me with my exam.

If you are praying for God to heal your body, pray, but then do something about it and go see the doctors and specialists that are out there to help you heal. Similarly, if you are praying to God to meet your financial needs, pray, but then do something about it. Read books, seek out successful men and women, and get their wise counsel.

Sit down and make a financial game plan together; don't waste time by doing nothing.

To summarize, we are not simply praying out of dependence upon God, but out of faith in God. If you really believe something, you will act in faith after you have prayed. God blesses our faith. We pray in faith, therefore, our prayers require action.

Karma Yoga is also heavily emphasized in the Bhagavad Gita.

How Karma Works

The Story of Two Sisters
There were once two sisters. The elder one was Preet, and the younger one was Bani. Both were completely different from each other in terms of nature and habits. Preet believed in God, but Bani didn't. Preet would wake up early in the morning, take a bath, and recite holy hymns. She was always working, whereas Bani would stay in bed sleeping and spend the entire day playing around.

Once they were traveling through the forest, Bani found a bag of coal. Bani was very happy to find that bag, as she could give it to their parents to sell and make some money.

As they walked further while talking about how lucky Bani was, Preet screamed with pain. It appeared that a splinter got stuck in Preet's foot.

While Preet was in pain, suddenly Bani started laughing.

Preet was surprised to see her laugh and asked, "Why are you laughing?"

Bani replied, "You've been worshipping God every day, and what you got as a result was a splinter in your foot, whereas I have never worshipped God, and yet I got a bag full of coal. Our parents are going to love me for this."

At that time, an old sage happened to pass by. The old sage heard Bani's comments and stopped near her. He had a big smile on his face. Bani was astonished to see that sage's smile.

Bani, with anger and confusion, asked the sage about the reason for his smile.

The old sage replied, "You are naive; you were destined to find a bag full of diamonds today if you had been worshiping God and doing good work, but you have only got a bag of coal."

Whereas your elder sister, Preet, was destined to be severely harmed but was splintered in her foot simply because she was worshiping God, severe physical loss was reduced to minor pain caused by a splinter. Moral:

We should live our lives doing good because God is always watching us and will always be there for us in our difficult times.

In Hinduism, there are three types of Karma.

Sanchit Karma (or Aprarabhda): The sum of all your previous karmas from previous lifetimes.

Prarabdha Karma: This encompasses the Karma you experience in this lifetime. (These are only a small part of the Sanchit Karma).

Agami Karma: The consequences of your current decisions and actions.

While I was growing up, my grandma told me Karma is like opening a bank account. We can choose how much money we want to put in to increase our balance or how much money we want to withdraw. We can choose to make different investments that result in interest to increase what we have available in our account. We can also choose to use credit, in which case we pay interest on what we spend. The choice is ours to make. Similarly, we have a karmic account. Each day we can choose whether we want to engage in thoughts, words, and deeds that are going to result in good that comes back to us. We can also engage in thoughts, words, and deeds for which we must pay the consequences.

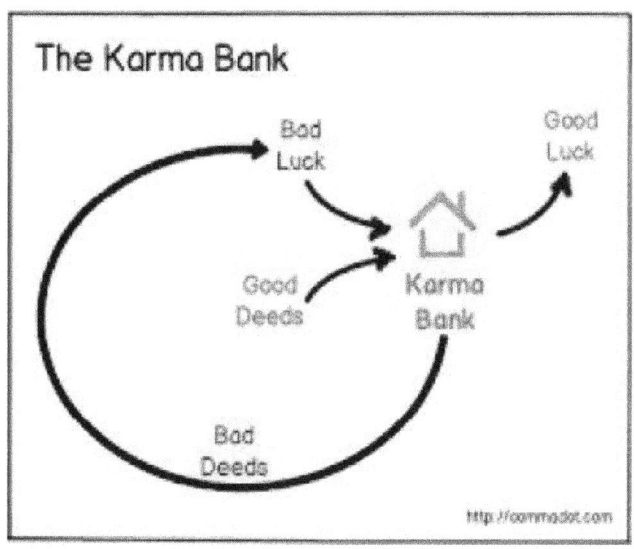

I believe praying to God and developing a relationship with him will automatically or effortlessly lead you to become a better person and will affect your actions in a positive way.

The theory of Karma is really vast and deep. I don't want to dig deep into it. We all don't know our previous birth karma, but what we do know about and are accountable for is our present life karma. So let us all try to be better humans. I know in this day and age it is not easy to become a goody two shoes. That is why Swami Vivekananda said the path of God-realization is very difficult, like walking on the edge of a sharp razor. Yet despair not; arise, despair not! Arise! Awake! And stop not till the goal is reached.

Teachings

No! No! I don't intend to scare anyone. All I want to say is that you start putting yourself under a big magnifying glass and scrutinizing yourself. That's what happened to me. I have a very innocent connection with God. I don't dwell much on rituals; it's more of a heartfelt connection. All through my growing age, I have been very conscious of myself, as I have mentioned before. I was conscious of the way I looked and the way I conducted myself. I always felt the need for acceptance and validation from people. I think my need for validation started at the tender age of 7 or 8 years. In my time, the environment we had in school always taught that only those children were worthy who excelled in everything.

Me trying to fit in led to me shutting down my true self and living in fear of not being accepted. I started hiding my flaws and became an introvert. My self-sabotaging behavior eroded my self-confidence and self-esteem, which affected my relationships as well. I don't want to touch base regarding how my lack of confidence in myself was affecting my relationship and life in general. Anyhow, all these things acted as catalysts to build my relationship with God. Now let me tell you how I felt the very first time when my grand-mother translated Punjabi Gurbani into Hindi from Gurugranth Sahib ji, which is in our Ghar Ka Mandir. Baba has been with us since the very first day my grandparents entered the house in 1965 (I must have been about 18 years old when I actually started understanding the meaning of Shabads in Gurbani). When dadi ma (grandmother) used to tell me the meaning of Gurubani in the evening during Samapti time or Sukhasan time, for me, that time was a blessing; I used to feel eternal bliss. It was like I had found peace through Gurbani. Itna Anand ata tha. I am now 30 years old, and the kind of emotions, the overwhelming feeling of bliss that I felt at the time, I haven't felt since. I'm still not sure how I became so connected at the time. Daddie used to say that I am able to take and enjoy His name (God's name) in this birth because of my pichle janam ka naam kamai.

The first thing I came to know about was "Ik Onkar," which is the first word of the moolmantra. The mool mantra is also significant because it is the opening text of the holy Sri Guru Granth Sahib, which contains the composition and bani of all the ten Sikh Gurus.

The mool mantra given by Sri Guru Nanak Dev is: "Ik Onkar Satnam, Karta Purakh, Nirbhau, Nirvair, Akal Murat, Ajuni Sai Bham, Guru Prasad."

This means: There's only one God; his name is the only truth; he is the only creator; he is fearless; he is without hate; he is immortal; he is beyond birth and death; and by only his grace, one can chant his name.

All of Sri Guru Nanak Dev Ji's teachings are contained in Guru Granth Sahib ji.

(Five teachings of Guru Nanak Dev ji that have changed my perspective on life.)

1. Vand Chhako: Sharing what God has given you with others and helping those who are in need.
2. Kirat Karo: To earn a living honestly. One should not exploit others to enjoy self-happiness. To make the teaching of Kirat Karo more impactful. My dadi ma told me a story of Bhai Lalo and Malik Bhago.

One day, Guru Nanak Dev Ji reached a place named Mardana. There lived a poor carpenter named Bhai Lalo. He invited Guru Nanak Dev Ji to his house for lunch. Guru Nanak Deviji accepted his invitation because everybody was equal to him; he had never differentiated between rich and poor, high and low caste, Hindus and Muslims, etc. On the other hand, Malik Bhago, a wealthy landlord of the village, also sent Guru Nanak Devji an invitation for lunch. With a lot of pride, Malik Bhago had prepared a massive feast for Guru Nanak Devji. Guru Nanak Devji sent a message to Bhai Lalo to join him at Malik Bhago's house. So Guru Nanak Devji went to Malik Bhago's house. There, Malik Bhago served a variety of tasty dishes for Guru Nanak Devji. Just then, Bhai Lalo arrived there with two makki rotis. Guru Nanak Devji took the Makki rotis and started eating them. Malik Bhago saw this, got offended, and asked, "Guruji." I've prepared a lavish feast for you, but you're eating his simple food from a poor man's hands. Is there something wrong I have done that you didn't consume my food? Hearing this, Nanak Devji took a piece of poori from Malik Bhago's dish in one hand and a piece of Bhai Lalo's makki roti in the other. He began squeezing the food, and something amazing happened. Out of Lalo's roti, milk came out! It was a miracle. But out of Malik Bhago's puri, drops of blood flowed. "Everyone was shocked," Malik Bhago arrogantly asked. "What does this prove?" Guruji smiled and said, "Malik Bhago, you exploit and torture the laborers who work and earn for you." You eat their blood; you treat them wrong. It's their blood that is flowing here. Bhai Lalo works hard and eats his own labor; thus, milk flows from his food. Malik Bhago, you should stop exploiting and suppressing the poor and the needy. True wealth lies in serving the poor. You will always be happy and prosperous if you do this."

Thus, Malik Bhago learnt a great lesson from Guru Nanak Devji and from then on he was devoted to his holy saint teacher Guru Nanak Devj.

3. Naam Japo: Chant the name of God. Sri Guru Nanak Devji emphasized meditating on God's name to gain control over the five evils: Kama, Krodh, Lobh, Moh, and ahankar, which mean lust, anger, greed, attachment, and ego.

Again, my dadi ma told me this beautiful Valmiki Ji story to instill the teachings of Naam Japo in me: Valmiki Ji was a highway robber named Ratnakara before becoming the famous sage who wrote the Ramayana. Everyone was afraid of Ratnakara. One day, the sage Narada was passing by the forest where Ratnakara lived. Seeing a good opportunity, Ratnakar attacked Narada to rob him. However, Narad remained unworried and calm. Ratnakara was in complete surprise because people trembled in fear upon hearing his name. Narada questioned Ratnakara as to why he was committing the sin of robbing others, to which Ratnakara replied, "To feed my family." On hearing this, Narada said, "Ratnakara, go and ask your family members if they will also share the sins you are committing to take care of them." After tying Narada to a tree to prevent him from escaping, Ratnakara returned to his family and asked his family members if they were willing to share his sin. No one was willing to share the burden of Ratnakara's sins. Heartbroken at his family's response, Ratnakara returned to Narada and asked him for the path of salvation. Narada then instructed him to chant the name of Lord Rama. But no matter how hard Ratnakara tried, he couldn't pronounce Rama. So Narada told him to pronounce Rama backwards as Mara.

Ratnakara began his meditation by chanting as Narada had instructed him to, but years passed. An ant hill grew all around and above him. Then he told Ratnakara that his meditation had paid off and God was pleased with him. Ratnakara was bestowed with the honor of Bramarishi and given the name of Valmiki since he was reborn from the Valmiki (the ant hill) and that is how he got his name Valmiki.

Even though Ratnakara chanted Rama as Mara with good intention. His mindset was changed to please God; therefore, he was successful in creating positive vibes around him by emitting positive energy. He was bestowed with the blessing of God, which cleaned up his bad deeds (Karma) and made him a holy saint.

4. Sarbat daa bhalaa: Ask the Lord for everyone's happiness. He said that despite religion, caste, and gender, everyone should seek well for others, and only then can one receive that goodness back in return.
5. Speak the truth without any fear: Sri Guru Nanak Devji said to always speak the truth without any fear.

Sri Guru Nanak Devji also laid great emphasis on the importance of having a guru in one's life. He said that without a true guru, one can never find God.

Coming back to why for me the path of spirituality became difficult like walking on a razor edge, I realised that I had placed myself under a large magnifying glass. I started judging myself. Now every wrongdoing—every desire, every bad thought, and every bad action—had caused me to feel remorse. I got stuck between doing right and doing wrong. I was so scared of hurting people or doing anything wrong because I thought my negative karma would hit me back. My limited mind was only thinking of what good I could do to avoid any suffering in life, as they say, "little knowledge is dangerous." I started suppressing my anger and my desires. I became god-fearing instead of God-loving at times when things wouldn't go my way, and I would question the existence of God. The confusion and turmoil within me suddenly clouded all the good thoughts. I am not sure if I am able to pin down the mental challenges that I have faced in my path of spirituality since the beginning.

I won't say I have overcome it yet, but I am still learning. For example, in our lives, we meet so many difficult people. When we are not aware of the enlightenment within us, we get angry. There are so many conflicts with those we do not like. Now when we suddenly get introduced to the idea of spirituality, we start looking at such things with a different perspective, and we are more mature when handling difficult situations. But not always. Being part of this material world with so much negativity around us, we tend to go back to our old selves and get back into a conflicting mode again. For me, it is like juggling between two worlds. I am in the middle of both worlds. Sometimes I used to find that when I tried to be extra nice and more accepting of people, people often took me for granted. I started feeling completely lost and alone. I became more aware of my old negative habits.

When bad things happened in my life, I began blaming myself and feeling guilty. Thinking, this is happening to me because I might have done something wrong. For me it was like I am having faith in God so my journey of life has to be smooth. The motive was selfish. I became weak. I was not able to overcome my desires and attachments.

I went into depression; yes, my confusion and my thoughts led me into a dark pit. I was not able to connect with myself, with my loved ones, or with God.

How I am overcoming my spiritual challenges

Firstly, I started with doing my duty without thinking about the results. It did not come easy; it is a natural human tendency that people focus more on the result than on the work. But I learned it because whenever I did a good deed, I always had the intention that if I did good, only good things would happen to me, and when something bad happened in my life, it made me wonder what the point of doing good karma was. It came to a point when my frustration level reached its peak. Then, like always, I had a one-on-one conversation with God. What is the point of being good if nothing good is ever going to happen to me? Suddenly it occurred to me, which I interpret as an answer from God, that whatever bad is happening to me could be the result of my past lives' deeds, over which I have no control in this life, but if I continue doing good, without actually thinking about the results, my efforts will not go to waste, and doing good acts will become my nature; they will no longer require efforts, and my life will slowly and gradually change for the better. Or another thing could be that I need to trust God; if my efforts are not rewarded, then there has to be a bigger reason. All these thoughts were pacifying and also helped me change my perspective to just focus on my work.

Okay! Let me put it in a better way:

The god of death, YAMRAJ, has an accountant called CHITRAGUPTA who keeps a record of all deeds. This record determines the circumstances of our future lives: the parents we shall have, the gender we shall acquire, the country in which we will be born, the difficulties and comforts we shall experience, etc. Our current life is a result of what we have done in our past lives. You have another chance to change your future in this life!

So do good today without thinking about the results, and your tomorrow will consequently turn out better?

"Results happen over time, not overnight. Work hard, stay consistent, and be patient."

– **Gymaholic**

Let Me Explain This More:
In simple terms, suppose you go to the office and work. Whether a company makes profit or loss, you get a salary, right? Similarly, consider that the world/life is an office. Work = your duty as per varna/ashram. You may succeed or win at times, but you may also fail or lose. But as long as you do your duty according to the shastras, you get a salary, which is moksha.

Material Meaning
Basically, "don't think of reward" means two things on a material level:

6. Don't lose hope or enthusiasm, even if you know that the probability of failure is higher than that of success.

7. Don't become overconfident and hasty just because you know that the probability of success is higher than that of failure.

I stopped fearing making mistakes in life. I came across this quote: "Sometimes, good people make bad choices. It doesn't mean they are bad people; it means they are human". I stopped putting myself in front of a big magnifying glass. I realized that maintaining a balance between spirituality and materialism is very important.

Materialism is inevitable. Senses and desires cannot be ignored. They have to be satisfied at the right level. If senses and desires are fundamental parts of human nature, then why ignore them? We have been born on this earth to live a full life, not just prepare to die.

Materialism is necessary, but its excess is clearly a problem. Spirituality helps us center ourselves and connect with our inner self. Spirituality can provide a deeper perspective and moral compass that can help balance the excess of materialism.

I accepted suffering as an integral part of life. Acceptance simply means that you stop trying to deny your reality and instead acknowledge it. Acceptance does not mean you approve of a situation or that you don't want it to change. Once we accept reality, our anger tends to decrease, and the painful situation loses the power it has over us. Suffering gives us a greater appreciation of the moments of comfort. If life were comfortable 24/7, we wouldn't be able to appreciate the moments of comfort. Wisdom emerges from the experience of suffering. When things go well, we rarely stop to ask questions about our lives. A difficult situation, however, often forces us out of our mindless state, causing us to reflect on our experiences.

In my case, I faced depression and had to deal with certain circumstances that were not in my control. I would often question God, "Why me?" I was frustrated and angry with God, but nobody around me could understand my problem because, although physically fit and fine from the outside, from the inside I was ill. I was in desperate need of help, in spite of all my anger and despair toward God. One thing I knew was that God is "omniscient." I realized the suffering I am getting today is leading me to a better tomorrow because I am God's child and he won't do anything to harm me.

All I need is faith in him. Something in me knew he wouldn't let me fall. Whatever suffering or hardship I am facing or will face in the future will make me resistant and better able to endure hardship. Just as a muscle, in order to build up, must endure some pain, so our emotions must endure pain in order to strengthen. Only through the experience of trial and suffering can the soul be strengthened, the vision cleared, the ambition inspired, and success achieved. Pain and joy are both parts of life. If you only get happiness, you won't understand the value of happiness. Suffering causes our focus to turn inward and face those parts of ourselves that we would otherwise ignore. Through suffering, compassion arises. But the only way we can gain a deep awareness of the suffering of others is by having suffered ourselves.

I am not saying that you go out and seek suffering. We don't ought to seek it actively just as the fact that sickness actually strengthens our immune system does not imply that we are ready to look for opportunities to become sick.

In our lives, we will get ample opportunities without actively looking for them to fortify our immune system.

The first of the Buddha's four noble truths is the truth of suffering, a truth we can either reject or accept as an inevitable part of being human. And when we learn to accept, even embrace, difficult experiences, our suffering becomes a tool, as an instrument for growth.

I started doing meditation. For me, meditation was very important. It is like hitting the pause button and bringing my awareness to the present moment. Meditation for me was just not confined to sitting still, closing eyes, and chanting. I could only do this for a maximum of 10 minutes. So what other form of meditation could I do? I realized that "while I dance, I cannot judge, I cannot hate, and I cannot separate myself from life." I can only be joyful and whole. I have never felt so safe, free, and present as I do now. I felt all of it because of the dance. It became my meditation and my relaxation. I asked myself what else I could do to bring my mind into the present moment. Then I took up writing. Writing down our thoughts can be a way to practice being present with whatever arises. I don't judge or censor what I write at that time. Whatever I write comes straight from my heart. Writing can be done by maintaining a journal. A journal is a place where you can regularly debrief and unload. It's a deeper form of detoxing the mind. I think of my journal as my compost bin. It's where I dump things to let them stew until they turn into something else.

A regular journaling practice can help you identify thought patterns and make you more aware of your reactions. If you do it regularly, it can train you to pause before you respond. A journal also gives you the luxury of a blank page. It's a clutter-free space where you can get to what's essential and to what should be a priority. It's not important whether you do this by hand or on your computer. Though writing by hand connects you in a different way to your mind because it forces you to slow down. Even if you think of your handwriting as ugly or if you haven't written by hand for a while, try it and see what it feels like.

Timed free writing in response to prompts is a very effective way of silencing the inner critic. Writing to a timer allows you to connect to your unfiltered voice, beyond your logical mind. It's a way of opening the door to the hidden cupboard with your mental clutter.

Set your timer for 10 minutes and write without stopping to think or edit. Just keep the pen moving, trusting that it will lead you to the heart of what is really bothering you. Here are my favourite prompts:

What scares me …

What worries me …

What I can let go

What if...

The key to using writing as a way to declutter the head is to do it regularly. Can you imagine living in a house that's permanently spring-cleaned? How blissful would that be? Take it from me. Living in a clutter-free home is liberating. It has made me a happier, more productive person. But just like my home requires constant cleaning, my mental clutter needs to be unloaded regularly to make sure I remain focused and clear about my goals and priorities. I couldn't imagine my life without regular writing practice.

Singing is also a form of meditation. If you sit and sing, you can feel it in your chest; you can feel parts of your body vibrating, and it's a pleasant feeling. It tends to help the muscles relax, helps the tightness and the constriction we feel when we get a lot of anxiety or stress from tension.

Alexander Devan Via Mindful

Painting is also a form of meditation.

Anyone can do art meditation, even if you think you aren't creative or if traditional meditation isn't their thing.

What also keeps me connected to the path of God is my grip on the reality that time does not remain the same. Sometimes there is joy, and sometimes there is sorrow. God has perfect timing, never early or late; it takes a little patience and a lot of faith, but it's worth the wait.

I know having patience is not easy when things don't go as planned; even my patience goes for a toss. But to regain my patience, I talk to God, I pour my heart out, I get angry, and I cry like a baby. It's natural, and I don't want to feel guilty about it. When I am done venting to God, I start feeling light at heart, as if God has given me the strength to wait and trust his process.

Something in me changes, making me feel safe, happy, and powerful. The voice inside me says all is well. Everything is working out for my highest good. Out of this situation, only good will come. This will work miracles in your life.

Gratitude is a special gift from God that brings happiness. When we express and receive gratitude, our brain releases dopamine and serotonin, the two crucial neurotransmitters responsible for our emotions, and they make us feel good. They enhance our mood immediately, making us feel happy from the inside. Gratitude is what makes our good days feel even better, but more importantly, it is the tool that gets us through the bad days. Don't get me wrong. I am not suggesting that gratitude will come easily or naturally in a crisis. We don't have total control over our emotions. We cannot easily allow ourselves to feel grateful, less depressed, or happy talking about me. I have gone through severe anxiety that has led to depersonalization and derealization disorder. I started feeling numbness in my mind, as if my senses were turned off, and I felt detached from myself, as if I had no actual self. I felt like a wall of glass was in front of me that separated me from the world. It was like I could see what was beyond the glass wall but was not able to connect. For me, it was difficult to attach emotion to memories. I felt so disconnected from everything. These symptoms of mental anxiety started taking a toll on my daily life. That's when I realized the importance of human emotions. I became numb in the sense that I craved to feel the emotions of love, happiness, sadness, and anger. Life became a straight line for me, with no desires. All I prayed for was to overcome the anxiety disorder.

Most of the time, it became so frustrating that I would ask God why I was even living. What I want to say is that during this time, I realized the importance of human emotions and life in general, which otherwise I would often take for granted. Then I realized how blessed I was to have no mental health issues.

Well, when times are good, people take prosperity for granted and begin to believe that they are invulnerable. In times of uncertainty, though, people realize how powerless they are to control their own destiny. If you begin to see that everything you have, everything you have counted on, may be taken away, it becomes much harder to take it for granted, so a crisis can make us more grateful. Maybe I wasn't a grateful person. God gave me such sufferings to make me realize what I have, count my blessings, and learn to be grateful from then on. I was grateful for even the smallest things in life. Remember, your goal is not to relive the experience but rather to get a new perspective on it. Learn to reframe. In bad situations, for example, if you didn't get the job you really wanted, instead of looking at the situation as an afterthought or a total failure, you can reframe it to look at it as an opportunity to brush up on your current skills or expand your knowledge. I am also learning to appreciate the little things in life. Be it good or bad, everything God does is for our own good. This reminds me of the story of Akbar and Birbal.

Birbal was a wise advisor of the emperor Akbar; he followed Akbar everywhere, and his favourite advice was "Everything happens for the good."

Once on a fine morning, Akbar decided to go hunting along with Birbal, and while he was hunting, he accidentally cut his finger with his sword. He asked Birbal what he thought about the accident, to which Birbal smiled and replied, "Everything happens for the good." This time, Akbar got very angry and ordered soldiers to put Birbal in prison. Akbar went to see Birbal in prison and said, "Now what do you think?" Do you still believe it? "Everything happens for good," to which Bribal replied yes. "I still believe everything happens for the good." So Birbal remained in prison. The next day, with his bandaged finger, Akbar again went to the forest for hunting with his soldiers. Akbar got separated from his soldiers and was captured by the tribes, who decided to offer him as a sacrifice to their God. While they were about to chop off his head, they saw that his finger was wounded, so they decided to throw him back to the jungle as per their custom; they cannot offer an imperfect body as a sacrifice to their God. His wounded finger became the reason for his release and thus saved his life.

On his return, he learned that Birbal was right and thanked God for hurting his finger. He immediately went to Birbal and asked for an apology, telling him that he was right. He also asked how his imprisonment was good for him, to which Birbal replied that if he had not been imprisoned, he would have accompanied Akbar to the forest, and when Akbar was rejected by the tribals, he would have been sacrificed to the tribal God in place of Akbar.

Whatever happens in life happens for good. Every incident in life has a connection to future incidents, which we are not able to see at that point in time. We are only able to relate it back once that connecting future incident happens. When we connect those past incidents, we realize their significance. Therefore, we should always be optimistic and look at the bright side of things.

The story also inspires people to practice gratitude in their daily lives. Whatever happens, we should be thankful for what we have instead of getting sad about what we have lost. Mulling over the bad part will only put you in a spiral of negative thoughts and bring more negativity into your life. Get over or let go of the things that were not in your control; focus on the positive side of them and look at them with wholeness. Learn from past mistakes because every challenge we face in life is for our own learning.

Well, I know how the human brain functions. It's not always easy to find light in the darkness. Our human brain is more fixated on the negative than on the positive aspects. In the best of times, our brain is conditioned to look for the downside in every situation, but during times of struggle and uncertainty, this negativity first tendency gets dialled up even further. To look for positivity or light, it's very important to embrace darkness or negativity. Whether that darkness comes in the form of a bad mood, negative emotion, or a difficult time in our life, darkness makes us uncomfortable, uneasy, fearful, and anxious, and because of all this, we try to ignore it, hide it in the deepest part of ourselves, hoping it will just go away. But this never works. The universe/God makes sure that what you resist persists, meaning that the more you resist anything in life, the more you bring it to you. Dwell deep into your soul, bring your inner negativity to the surface, and transform it into positivity. Life's pain and confusion must be acknowledged, but if we don't balance that with the same positive emotions of pleasure, we are going to burn out quickly. Managing negative emotions is more about embracing the fact that we are feeling them, determining why we are feeling this way, and allowing ourselves to receive the messages that they are sending us before we release them and move forward.

Not only are negative emotions a natural part of life, but they are that way for a good reason. Fear, anger, hurt, rejection — all these feelings are useful emotional responses to certain situations. For example, fear helps us survive. Without fear, we'd be crossing the road without looking. We wouldn't think twice about walking alone through a dodgy part of town in the middle of the night. We'd get ourselves into all kinds of physically dangerous situations.

Sometimes these feelings crop up in inopportune or unwanted situations. For example, we might feel the same kind of fear when we think about public speaking as we do when we imagine scaling Everest. The solution isn't to never feel fear, though. Instead, it's to learn how to manage it so it can serve its natural purpose.

Quotes For Uplifting Your Mood In Hard Times

Sharing A Few Quotes That Keep Me Going During My Hard Times

1. God says, "Remember these four things."
2. I will make a way for you.
3. I am fighting your battles.
4. Prayer is the best medicine.
5. Trust my timing.
6. One day, it's all going to be clear. It's all going to make sense, and you're going to be able to say, "So that's why God allowed that in my life!" Until then, God wants you to trust Him. (**Rick Warren**)
7. Dukh main sumiran sab kare, sukh main kare na koye Jo sukh me sumiran kare, toh dukh kahe ko hoye.

Sant Kabir Ji Ka Doha

(We all think of the Lord when we are troubled, never when we are at peace, but if we hold our faith during peace, there would be no trouble.)

8. "One must first conquer one's own evils and wrong habits." --Guru Nanak Dev ji

9. "If you keep thinking only about the future, then you will also lose the present."

Guru Nanak Dev Ji

10. Prayer is more powerful than your obstacles.

11. Everyone has to do Karma in order to get fruits on the land of Karam. God gives only lines but we have to fill them with color – **Guru Nanak Dev ji**

12. Don't forget that you are human; it's okay to have a meltdown. Just don't unpack and live there. Cry it out, and then refocus on where you are headed.

13. Check yourself—sometimes you are a toxic person. Sometimes you are the mean, negative person; you're looking to push away. Sometimes the problem is you. And that does not make you less worthy to keep on growing. Keep on checking yourself. Keep on motivating yourself; mistakes are opportunities. Look at them, own them, grow from them, and move on. Do better, be better. You're human. It's okay.

14. Sometimes, we are tested not to show our weaknesses but to discover our strengths.

15. Teri kismat da likha, tere toh koi kho nahi sakda. Je usdi meher hove to tenu oh vi mil jaaye, jo tera ho nahi sakda-Guru Ranth Sahib

16. Make someone smile every day, but never forget that you're someone too.

17. There are two ways to live: you can live as if nothing is a miracle, or you can live as if everything is a miracle.

(Albert Einstein)

18. Begin to live as though your prayers are already
19. Do not blame anyone else; instead, your own actions are to be blamed. Whatever I did, I have suffered, and I do not blame anyone else.

Guru Nanak Dev ji

For My Readers

I want to end this book by dedicating a song to the one who feels like giving up.

This is my go to song to lift my spirits.

Dhundhla jaayein jo manzilein

Ik pal ko tu nazar jhuka

Jhuk jaayein sar jahan wahin

Milta hai rab ka raasta

Teri qismat tu badal de

Rakh himmat bas chal de

Tere saathi, mere kadmon ke hain nishaan

Tu na jaane aas paas hai khuda

Meaning: It is the destination to get hazy, lower your sight for a moment, wherever your head is bowed down, there only the way to God is found, you change your luck. Be strong; just start moving. My footprints are your companion. You don't know God is nearby.

Khud pe daal tu nazar Halaton se haarkar kahan chala re

Haath ki lakeer ko modta marodta hai hausla re

To khud tere khwabon ke rang mein

Tu apne jahan ko bhi rang de

Ke chalta hoon main tere sang mein

Ho shaam bhi to kya

Jab hoga andhera Tab paayega dar mera

Us dar pe phir hogi teri subah

Tu na jaane aas paas hai khuda

Meaning: see yourself, lost, against circumstance, where your lines of palm are turned and twisted by courage. In the color of your dreams, color your world too, I walk with you. Even in the evening, when it's dark, you'll find my door. Your morning will be there on that door; you don't know God is nearby.

Mit jaate hain sabke nishan

Bas ek woh mitta nahi hai haaye...

Maan le jo har mushkil ko marzi meri haaye

Ho humsafar na tera jab koi

Tu ho jahan rahunga mein wahin

Tujhse kabhi na ik pal bhi mein juda Tu na jaane aas paas hai Khuda

Meaning: – Signs of everyone get erased. The only one who doesn't get erased, is the one who takes every problem as my will. When you have no companion, I'll be there where you are. Even for a moment, I am not far from you. You don't know that God is nearby.

P.S. Remember to keep praying; God is listening.

Kritika Khetarpal Malik

Prayer journal

Date: __/__/____

Today I'm grateful For:

People To Pray For:

Self Imrovement:

Answers to Prayer/ Hand of God in my life today:

SHORT TERM REQUESTS:
-
-
-
-
-

LONG TERM REQUESTS:
-
-
-
-
-

Date : __/__/____

People To Pray For :

Today I'm grateful For:

Self Imrovement:

Answers to Prayer/ Hand of God in my life today:

SHORT TERM REQUESTS:
-
-
-
-
-

LONG TERM REQUESTS:
-
-
-
-
-

Date: __/__/____

People To Pray For:

Today I'm grateful For:

Self Imrovement:

Answers to Prayer/ Hand of God in my life today:

SHORT TERM REQUESTS:
-
-
-
-
-
-

LONG TERM REQUESTS:
-
-
-
-
-
-

Date : __/__/____

People To Pray For :

Today I'm grateful For:

Self Imrovement:

Answers to Prayer/ Hand of God in my life today:

SHORT TERM REQUESTS:
-
-
-
-
-
-

LONG TERM REQUESTS:
-
-
-
-
-
-

Keep Praying God Is Listening

Date: __/__/____

People To Pray For:

Today I'm grateful For:

Self Imrovement:

Answers to Prayer/ Hand of God in my life today:

SHORT TERM REQUESTS:
-
-
-
-
-

LONG TERM REQUESTS:
-
-
-
-
-

Date: __/__/____

People To Pray For:

Today I'm grateful For:

Self Imrovement:

Answers to Prayer/ Hand of God in my life today:
_____
_____
_____
_____
_____
_____
_____
_____
_____
_____
_____
_____

SHORT TERM REQUESTS:
-
-
-
-
-
-

LONG TERM REQUESTS:
-
-
-
-
-
-

Date: __/__/____

Today I'm grateful For:

People To Pray For:

Self Imrovement:

Answers to Prayer/ Hand of God in my life today:

SHORT TERM REQUESTS:

-
-
-
-
-
-

LONG TERM REQUESTS:

-
-
-
-
-
-

Date: __/__/____

Today I'm grateful For:

People To Pray For:

Self Imrovement:

Answers to Prayer/ Hand of God in my life today:

SHORT TERM REQUESTS:
-
-
-
-
-
-

LONG TERM REQUESTS:
-
-
-
-
-
-

Date: __/__/____

People To Pray For:

Today I'm grateful For:

Self Imrovement:

Answers to Prayer/ Hand of God in my life today:

SHORT TERM REQUESTS:
-
-
-
-
-
-

LONG TERM REQUESTS:
-
-
-
-
-

Date: __/__/____

People To Pray For:

Today I'm grateful For:

Self Imrovement:

Answers to Prayer/ Hand of God in my life today:

SHORT TERM REQUESTS:

-
-
-
-
-
-

LONG TERM REQUESTS:

-
-
-
-
-
-

www.ingramcontent.com/pod-product-compliance
Lightning Source LLC
LaVergne TN
LVHW061345080526
838199LV00094B/7371